AL-KINDI

The Father of Arab Philosophy

Great Muslim Philosophers and Scientists of the Middle Ages ™

AL-KINDI

The Father of Arab Philosophy

Tony Abboud

rosen
central ™

The Rosen Publishing Group, Inc., New York

Published in 2006 by The Rosen Publishing Group, Inc.
29 East 21st Street, New York, NY 10010

Library of Congress Cataloging-in-Publication Data

Abboud, Tony.
Al-Kindi: the father of Arab philosophy/Tony Abboud.—1st ed.
    p. cm.—(Great Muslim philosophers and scientists of the Middle Ages)
ISBN 1-4042-0511-X (library binding)
1. Kindi, d. ca. 873. 2. Philosophy, Arab. 3. Philosophy, Medieval. 4.
Philosophy and religion.
I. Title. II. Series.
B753.K5423 2006
181'.6—dc22

2005022428

Manufactured in the United States of America

On the cover: Portrait of al-Kindi.

CONTENTS

Introduction

A PIONEERING ARAB THINKER

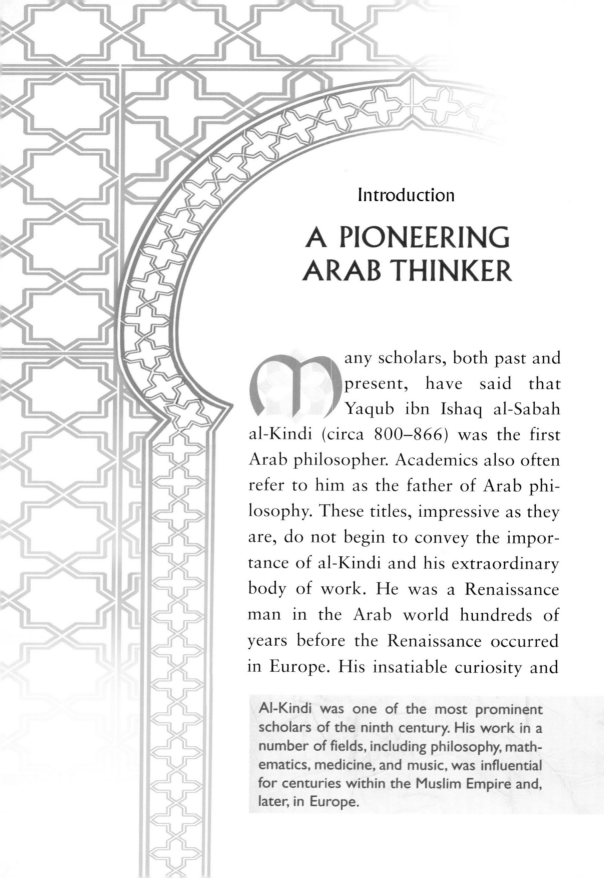

Many scholars, both past and present, have said that Yaqub ibn Ishaq al-Sabah al-Kindi (circa 800–866) was the first Arab philosopher. Academics also often refer to him as the father of Arab philosophy. These titles, impressive as they are, do not begin to convey the importance of al-Kindi and his extraordinary body of work. He was a Renaissance man in the Arab world hundreds of years before the Renaissance occurred in Europe. His insatiable curiosity and

Al-Kindi was one of the most prominent scholars of the ninth century. His work in a number of fields, including philosophy, mathematics, medicine, and music, was influential for centuries within the Muslim Empire and, later, in Europe.

quest for knowledge meant that virtually all known subjects of his time fell within his expert capabilities.

During his life, al-Kindi wrote between 200 and 270 books and papers. Many of these have been lost, and researchers have not yet translated all of the existing texts into Western languages. Only in recent decades have the majority of his works begun to resurface. These works shed light on al-Kindi's teachings and theories. Al-Kindi tried to reconcile some of the differences that have severed the Eastern and Western countries for millennia. On one side, there were religious views and ideologies that emerged from the Arabic culture. On the other were somewhat corresponding views linked primarily to the Greeks. Civilization at the time of al-Kindi was in its relative infancy. However, many people continued to search for the "truth" about life, nature, science, and human behavior from any reliable source, no matter its cultural origins. Al-Kindi exemplified this open-mindedness to other cultures, which even today is a very rare quality.

To imagine the world he lived in, one must travel back to when ancient Greece culturally dominated the Mediterranean region and surrounding areas. Most anthropologists today believe that humans originated in Africa and traveled to nearby lands that could support population growth through proper water and food sources. With its water-fed Fertile Crescent, Mesopotamia, which included the modern-day region of Iraq, was one such place. In fact, many historians believe that the biblical Garden of Eden, with its lush foliage and beautiful plants, existed in what is now Iraq. Greece and its islands formed another place of early human settlement.

For thousands of years, before Rome's dominance at around 146 BC, Greece flourished. Economic and political stability, combined with advanced methods of scholarship and social organization, created a rich environment within ancient Greece that produced numerous philosophers, scientists, and other academics, such as Socrates (ca. 470–399 BC), Plato (ca. 428–347 BC), and Aristotle (384-322 BC). The teachings of these men remain influential today. Al-Kindi revered their work and desired to introduce what were called the foreign sciences to the Arabs.

The Arabs, however, had also evolved their own culture. While agriculture likely originated around the Fertile Crescent near central Persia, many surrounding areas were in the desert. An entirely different lifestyle, therefore, evolved in the region, which is today known as the Middle East. Nomadic tribes took their families and animal herds across the desert landscape. This way of living led to certain traditions and spiritual beliefs that mirrored the Arabic way of life. Westerners did not understand many Arab regulations and traditions.

This ignorance in the West, combined with the Arabs' own desire to establish a distinctive culture, contributed to the East-West divide. The Arabs did not completely trust views

The expansion of the Muslim Empire in the seventh through ninth centuries made the intellectual products of ancient and conquered cultures available to Muslim scholars such as al-Kindi. This map shows the reach of the empire around 700, seven decades after the death of the prophet Muhammad, and around 850, when al-Kindi was one of its most prominent citizens.

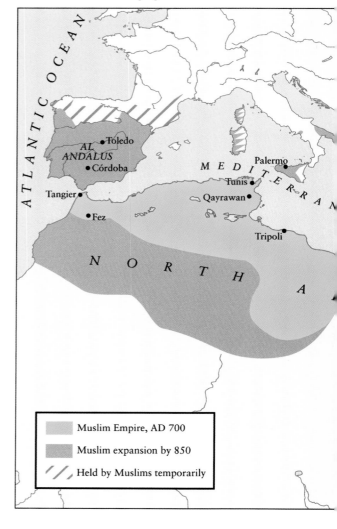

ATLANTIC OCEAN

AL ANDALUS

Toledo

Córdoba

MEDITERRANEAN

Palermo

Tunis

Tangier

Qayrawan

Fez

Tripoli

NORTH A

	Muslim Empire, AD 700
	Muslim expansion by 850
	Held by Muslims temporarily

from ancient Greece, Rome, and existing Jewish settlements. This mistrust carried over to the works of the Greek scholars, who were respected in many other parts of the world. Al-Kindi, however, had the wisdom to see through the prejudice on both sides. He took the best of both worlds and united them together in his own writings.

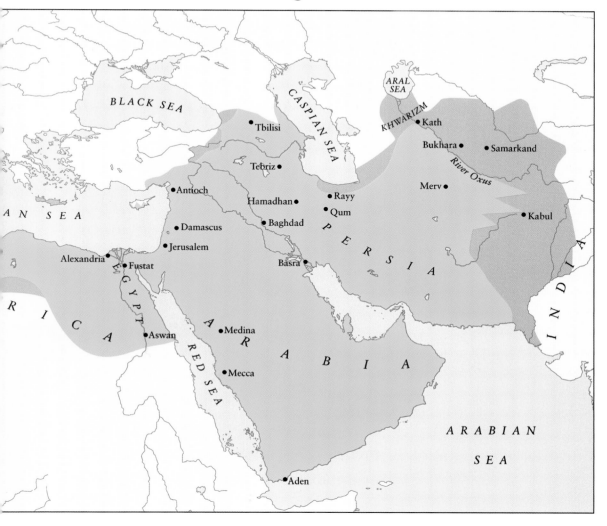

Al-Kindi studied the Greek works and was able to bridge the gap between the West and the East. That alone would make his work relevant today, but he also brought his own unique voice to his writings. Al-Kindi was an Arab, but, like the Greek philosophers before him, his work belongs to the world for all readers to experience and to enjoy.

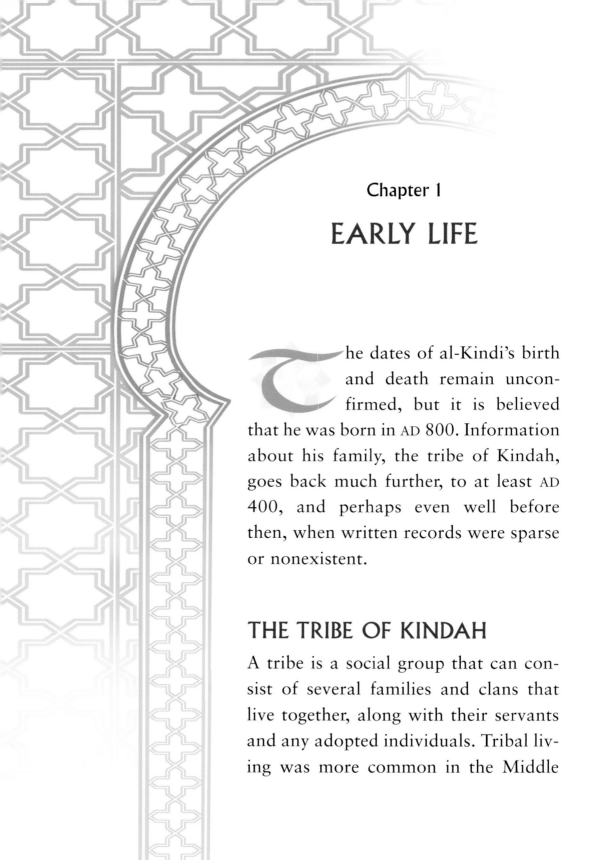

Chapter 1

EARLY LIFE

The dates of al-Kindi's birth and death remain unconfirmed, but it is believed that he was born in AD 800. Information about his family, the tribe of Kindah, goes back much further, to at least AD 400, and perhaps even well before then, when written records were sparse or nonexistent.

THE TRIBE OF KINDAH

A tribe is a social group that can consist of several families and clans that live together, along with their servants and any adopted individuals. Tribal living was more common in the Middle

The Hadramawt mountain range, where al-Kindi's tribe originated, can be seen in the background of this aerial view of the city of Shibam, Yemen. A relatively low mountain range, its highest peak is approximately 8,000 feet (2,440 meters).

East and Far East, where communities of related family members tended to stick together in unified groups. In China, for example, some early housing complexes consisted of apartment-like buildings that exclusively housed members of a single family over many generations.

Given the nomadic life of the Arabs, tribal living made sense. Men, women, and children could contribute to the family unit without necessarily being tied to a certain city or location. The tribe of Kindah originated in the mountains of Hadramawt in Yemen. This area is on the Arabian Peninsula. It is unknown when the first members of Kindah were born, but it must have been close to the first century AD or beforehand, given the tribe's later prominence.

During the fifth and the sixth centuries AD, the tribe of Kindah wielded considerable cultural and political influence. One of the greatest poets of the Arab world before the age of Islam was Amara al-Qais, who was a Kindah tribal member. The tribe also helped to unite all people living on the Arabian Peninsula, chiefly because of the Kindah contribution to language. Members of the Kindah tribe promoted the idea that a single language, Arabic, should be used among all people in the region. While some individuals could speak more than one language, such an ability was rare and translators were not as common then as they are today. Communication and any kind of central organization required the adoption of a single language. Due to the efforts of the Kindah tribe, the Arabs were poised to join together during the sixth century.

MUHAMMAD

It was during this critical period of unification along the Arabian Peninsula that one of the world's most influential religious leaders was born. The prophet Muhammad

(AD 570–632) was born in the city of Mecca (Makkah). He, too, was a member of a desert tribe (Quraysh). According to Islam, which is based on the Qur'an (also known as the Koran) and the teachings of Muhammad, the Prophet was drawn to religion in 610, when, at forty years old, he had a dramatic experience while he was meditating in a cave on Mount Hira. According to the Islamic faith, the angel Gabriel, mentioned in the Bible, called upon Muhammad to serve as a prophet and to share God's message to all people. Muhammad began to preach publicly throughout Mecca.

At first, Muhammad's message appealed to poorer members of society. Later, members of Mecca's aristocracy began to join him. The Quraysh elders grew hostile to Muhammad and the early followers of Islam, known as Muslims. Muhammad moved to Medina, where he was welcomed. Muhammad became the city's leader, and created a pact between the Muslims, Jews, and tribes in the area against the Quraysh. Muhammad had also hoped that the Jews would accept him as a prophet. However, many Jewish tribes allied with the Meccans instead, believing them to be stronger. Over time, the Muslims prevailed in a series of battles with the Quraysh, and Mecca surrendered to Muhammad. Muhammad cleared the Kabah, an ancient temple in Mecca, of hundreds of idols that the Arabs had kept there, and declared it the House of God. Muslims face towards the Kabah during their daily prayers.

This illustration portrays Muhammad *(fourth from right)*, accompanied by his key followers, addressing a delegation of Christians and Jews in Nadjan (in present-day Yemen). For some time, Muhammad maintained a warm relationship with Jews and Christians, and he saw his mission as an extension of the careers of their earlier prophets.

Muhammad controlled most of Arabia at this point. Many Arab tribes pledged allegiance to him and accepted him as a prophet. The beliefs of Islam spread and further united the Arabs, who were already poised to join Islam due to the efforts of the Kindah tribe.

One of Muhammad's companions and chief advisers was, in fact, a member of the famous tribe. Al-Ashath ibn Qais, like many other prominent Arabs, adopted Islam as his religion and dedicated his life to Muhammad's pursuits. Al-Ashath ibn Qais later became al-Kindi's grandfather, so there is a direct link between al-Kindi and one of the world's most powerful, influential, and renowned prophets and teachers of spiritual and behavioral thought.

THE QUR'AN

The revelations from God to Muhammad, through the angel Gabriel, are said to be preserved in the Qur'an, which is to Muslims what the Torah and Bible are, respectively, to Jews and Christians. The Qur'an is the Muslim sacred text that followers of Islam read and recite in worship. Muslims believe that the revelations to Muhammad began at around AD 610 and ended upon the Prophet's death in 632. Believers treasure its words to such an extent that they feel the physical Qur'an on Earth duplicates a text that is stored in heaven.

Like the Bible, the Qur'an contains spiritual guidance and rules meant to govern everyday life. As a political leader, Muhammad accomplished many lasting deeds during his direct reign. He abolished the worship of idols. At the time, parents also slaughtered unwanted baby girls. Muhammad ended that cruel practice. He also made statements against polygamy, the practice of a person having many spouses at the same time, and he tried to limit instances of divorce. (According to some Muslim and Western scholars, Muhammad himself had several

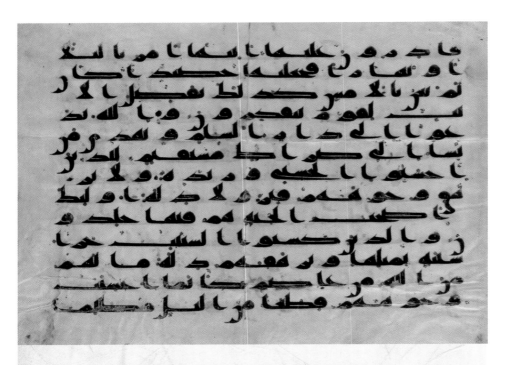

This is a page from a ninth-century copy of the Qur'an. It is written on parchment in the kufic script. (The script is named after the city of Kufa in southern Iraq.) The page shows verses from Jonah, the tenth sura (chapter), describing the pleasures that people who trust in Allah can expect.

wives during his lifetime.) He dedicated much of his work to promoting peace and nonviolence, except in cases of self-defense or for the empowerment of Islam. He also attempted to help the poor and to limit slavery, which was common in the ancient world. Many of these beliefs are upheld in the Qur'an, which also includes instructions concerning daily prayers and teachings that state that followers of Islam should be brave, humble, and just.

As with the Bible, it is almost impossible to comprehend the past and present importance of the Qur'an's influence. It provides the basis for all Islamic education and laws. It is also one of the most widely read books in the world. The Qur'an put the beliefs of the followers of Islam down on paper. Now, instead of just reading the works of other cultures, the Arabs had their own book to study and to contemplate. Later this text would be shared among Muslims all over the world.

Art and literature thrived within the Muslim Empire. This decorative dish from ninth-century Iraq is stamped with a verse from the Umayyad poet Muhammad Bashir ibn al-Khariji.

ISHAQ IBN AL-SABBAH

Shortly after the Arabs adopted the Qur'an as their official sacred text, al-Kindi's father, Ishaq ibn al-Sabbah, was born. He lived in the city of Kufa, which was established in Persia in 641. Initially it was just a camp for soldiers to rest, train, and regroup. Kufa later evolved into a vibrant urban center with shops and artisans that helped to define the emerging Arabic culture.

Al-Ashath ibn Qais, al-Sabbah's father, along with other followers of Muhammad, took his family to Kufa. There his relatives thrived amid the creative hustle and bustle of city life. Already wealthy and powerful due to the eminence of the Kindah tribe, al-Ashath ibn Qais enjoyed a prominent place in society. Eventually, Ishaq ibn al-Sabbah was named governor. He served under the reigns of two Abbasid caliphs.

HARUN AL-RASHID

After Muhammad, people called Muslim leaders caliphs. The first caliphs served as both religious and political leaders within Muslim society. On September 14, 786, Harun al-Rashid (763–809) became the fifth caliph of the Abbasid tribal dynasty. Harun al-Rashid was a pivotal leader whose decisions would set the stage for al-Kindi's later work.

A studious man, Harun al-Rashid supported intellectual pursuits, the arts, and the written legacy of the Greek scholars. He brought to his court experts in all major fields. One of these individuals was a scholar named Abul Husayn Muslim ibn al-Hajjaj Qushayri al-Nisaburi, or al-Hajjaj. His job was to translate into Arabic a book called *The Elements* by the Greek scientist and mathematician Euclid (ca. 325–265 BC). This translation was the first real step that the Arabs took toward understanding works that Arabs themselves had not

This miniature painting from a nineteenth-century manuscript portrays a confrontation between Abu Sufyan and al-Abbas, representing the prophet Muhammad, before the battle for Mecca in AD 630. Muhammad's conquest of the city is a milestone in Muslim history.

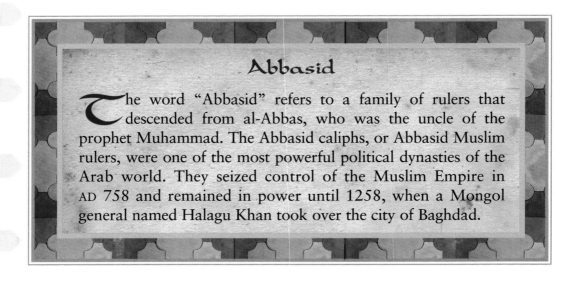

Abbasid

The word "Abbasid" refers to a family of rulers that descended from al-Abbas, who was the uncle of the prophet Muhammad. The Abbasid caliphs, or Abbasid Muslim rulers, were one of the most powerful political dynasties of the Arab world. They seized control of the Muslim Empire in AD 758 and remained in power until 1258, when a Mongol general named Halagu Khan took over the city of Baghdad.

written. It was a monumental move by Harun al-Rashid because it suggested that it was permissible for a follower of Islam to be interested in writings outside of the Muslim faith. Harun al-Rashid's openness to other cultures allowed al-Kindi and many other great Arabic scholars to work in relative freedom.

AL-KINDI'S CHILDHOOD AND EDUCATION

Approximately ten years before Harun al-Rashid's death, al-Kindi was born in Kufa. Very little is known about his earliest years, except that he memorized the Qur'an in its entirety, as most educated young men did. He also studied arithmetic and Arabic grammar and literature. Science and

This nineteenth-century illustration by Ambrose Dudley portrays Harun al-Rashid, the fifth caliph of the Abbasid dynasty, welcoming one of Holy Roman emperor Charlemagne's ambassador to his court in Baghdad. During his reign, Harun al-Rashid maintained strong diplomatic ties with the Holy Roman Empire and with China. His name means "Aaron the Just" in English.

philosophy, however, were his two favorite subjects. To further his studies, his family sent al-Kindi to Baghdad, which was the home of many scholars. In Baghdad, he was introduced to the written works of the Greeks. He also likely became fluent in Greek and Syrian languages, although information about his language studies has never been confirmed. It is clear, however, that he was able to read the works of Greek scholars, through either his own translations or those of other Arab colleagues. Al-Kindi refers to these texts in many of his own later works. Al-Kindi began work serving as tutor to the son of Caliph Mutasim (who reigned from 833 to 842 and whose full name was Ahmad Muhammad al-Mutasim). It was in Baghdad, both literally and figuratively, that al-Kindi found himself in a house of wisdom.

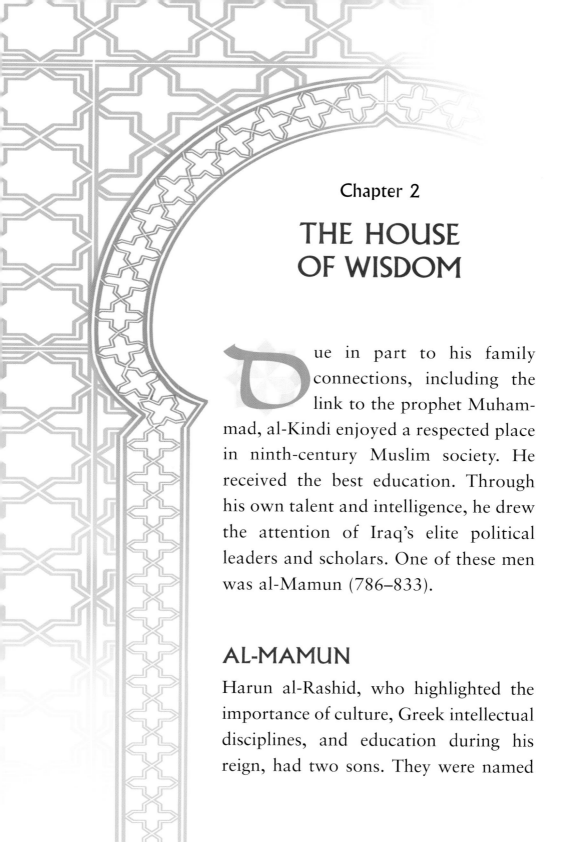

Chapter 2

THE HOUSE OF WISDOM

Due in part to his family connections, including the link to the prophet Muhammad, al-Kindi enjoyed a respected place in ninth-century Muslim society. He received the best education. Through his own talent and intelligence, he drew the attention of Iraq's elite political leaders and scholars. One of these men was al-Mamun (786–833).

AL-MAMUN

Harun al-Rashid, who highlighted the importance of culture, Greek intellectual disciplines, and education during his reign, had two sons. They were named

This sixteenth-century illustration from the *Khamsa* (Five Poems) by Persian poet Nizami portrays Caliph al-Mamun being groomed by a barber and other attendants *(center circle)*. The manuscript of verses builds ethical stories around traditional Muslim heroes such as al-Mamun.

al-Mamun and al-Amin. When Harun al-Rashid died, the two brothers vied for power. This kind of power struggle was common throughout most of the world until leadership by birth became less common. British kings and queens, for example, often had to fight with their siblings to gain control over the empire. Sometimes they would even imprison a brother or sister, or banish the individual to another country just to gain power.

In the case of the fight between al-Mamun and al-Amin, the struggle turned brutal. A mini war ensued with both men lining up their supporters to do battle. While the details of this battle remain undocumented, it is known that al-Amin was defeated and killed by al-Mamun and his men in the year 813.

Although his rule began violently, al-Mamun continued the good works of his father. Like Harun al-Rashid, al-Mamun respected men of learning. He continued to provide financial support for educational pursuits, which were favored in his court. Al-Mamun established observatories throughout his empire. These enabled astronomers to use the best equipment of the time. They also could receive pay, housing, and support from the court.

In the days before computers and electronic documents, the written word was revered. Imagine what it would have been like to live in one country but to desire the best books of another country and not have the benefit of airplanes, the Internet, telephones, or other forms of modern technology. During the ninth century, books and papers had to be memorized and then written down from an oral recitation. Or, they were physically copied and transported from one place to another, often over long distances. As such, libraries were quite rare.

Al-Mamun established one of the first great libraries of the Arab world. Such libraries had previously existed in ancient Egypt and Greece, but even they were subject to burning by enemy groups. For al-Mamun's library, which likely was one of the best since the famed Library of Alexandria, books and papers were collected at great effort from the city of Byzantium. These books were written in languages such as Greek, Latin, and Syriac. They would be of little use to those Arabs who spoke only Arabic. Al-Mamun also wished to further the teachings within these books, and to present them in ways that could be relevant to his people. To support these efforts and others, al-Mamun created the House of Wisdom.

THE ESTABLISHMENT OF THE HOUSE OF WISDOM

During al-Mamun's time, Baghdad was a major city. It had all of the comforts that people at the time would have relished, such as hospitals; shopping areas; museums; libraries; and places of worship, which Muslims call mosques. Many people today refer to this time as the golden age of Muslim civilization, because people from all over the world became aware of all of the Muslim achievements and were drawn to Baghdad, similar to how individuals today travel to the world's great cities for work, study, and pleasure.

Given its impressive roster of scholars, the House of Wisdom was undoubtedly the scene of great intellectual debates and discussions, as well as political wrangling. As such, it was part of a strong tradition of scholarship during the height of the Muslim Empire. This illustration from *The Maqamat* (The Assemblies) by eleventh-century author al-Hariri of Basra, portrays a literary meeting.

It was in Baghdad that al-Mamun established the Bayt al-Hikmah, which means "house of wisdom." Scholars from many different cultures and backgrounds traveled to Baghdad to work or to perform research at this impressive center for learning. Today, it would be somewhat comparable to places like Oxford University in England, the Sorbonne in France, or the Ivy League universities in the United States. However, even these impressive universities probably would have paled in comparison to the influence that the House of Wisdom had in its time. Such centers of learning were relatively rare in the 800s.

Today students rely upon certain classic works for different disciplines. Students of English, for example, usually read the plays and sonnets of Shakespeare (1564–1616). Students of evolutionary science read the books of Charles Darwin (1809–1882). In the ninth century, scholars and students heavily relied upon works by the respected Greek philosophers and scientists, whose works were the focus of study and translation at the House of Wisdom. These Greeks included Socrates, Plato, Aristotle, and Euclid, all of whom exerted great influence on al-Kindi.

SOCRATES

One of the earliest well-known Greek scholars, Socrates, was born around 470 BC and lived until about 399 BC. He wrote no books, but he gained fame as a public speaker and teacher. His greatest contributions were his philosophical views. Socrates believed in the power of knowledge. He claimed that virtue itself was knowledge and that men who knew what was right would act accordingly. He put more emphasis on rational thinking than on spiritual views or the ideals of the state. He promoted the idea that people should be able to think and to behave in a free manner, so long as they followed a rational, or reasoned, path.

Although Socrates himself was a deeply religious man and a patriot, many people associated with the government and religious orders thought his views were blasphemous. They charged Socrates with corrupting the minds of students against democracy, and accused him of worshipping gods not approved by the state. He was sentenced to death and forced to drink poison. By the time of his execution, however, Socrates had already spread his teachings to other influential men, including Plato.

PLATO

The distinguished pupil of Socrates, Plato lived from approximately 428 to 347 BC. In his early life, he was primarily educated in gymnastics and music, but he later became an expert on numerous other disciplines within the arts and sciences, including math, physics, astronomy, politics, ethics, aesthetics, poetry, painting, and sculpture. He founded a

In this famous oil painting, *The Death of Socrates* by Charles Alphonse Dufresnoy, the great Greek philosopher is about to drink the poison that will kill him, as required by the death sentence imposed on him for blasphemy. Socrates is portrayed as strong and confident even as he faces death, while his students avert their eyes in sadness and despair.

learning center within Athens called the Academy. It likely served as a model for the House of Wisdom.

At the Academy, Plato and other prominent educators taught their students about all major findings in the sciences and philosophy. The Academy made Athens the center for learning in Greece. For his teachings in philosophy, Plato took the ideas of Socrates and developed them a bit further. Plato believed in the theory of forms, which stresses the idea of something rather than the material object itself. For example, when a person views another individual, he or she sees the person based on preconceived notions. The idea, or memory, of the person remains, even though time may lead to changes. For example, you might remember a friend or an event from years ago, even though time has changed the actual person or the place.

Plato believed that ideas are eternal and unchangeable. He also thought they existed outside of normal reality, meaning that they somehow occupied a plane of existence that transcended what occurs in everyday life. This way of thinking was pivotal in the ancient world because it put emphasis on the importance of the mind and thought, which could both be shaped by education. It moved people toward independence as individuals, instead of just existing as a cog within a state's doctrinal or political machinery. It also influenced religious views because it put more emphasis on thought and prayer as opposed to action and the acquisition of material wealth. Al-Kindi adopted many of Plato's views in his own philosophical writings, but he particularly looked to Aristotle for inspiration.

ARISTOTLE

Just as Plato was a student of Socrates', Aristotle was a student of Plato's. Born to a physician father in about 384 BC,

This first-century Roman mosaic portrays scholars at the Academy, the school that Plato founded in Athens in 387 BC to provide a place where scholars could work. The Academy offered classes in philosophy, astronomy, mathematics, biology, and political theory. It remained in use until AD 529. Plato is widely regarded as one of the most important Western philosophers. His best-known work is *The Republic*.

Aristotle admirably followed in his teacher's path. He wound up opening his own school, called the Lyceum, around 335 BC. Through his teachings and writings, Aristotle hoped to harmonize all human experience. Every subject was of interest to him. He wrote well-known books on astronomy, meteorology, plants, animals, and more.

His philosophical theories were built on those of Plato. Aristotle shared Plato's belief that ideas are important, but he put more emphasis on the notion that thought can lead to action, or to something more concrete. For example, a person may have the talent to draw. That is possessed in the individual's mind and body. The person can then tap into that talent by using it to produce a work of art. As a result, Aristotle was one of the first philosophers to address the idea of cause and effect. Everything, he thought, begins with a cause that produces an effect. This basic principle was applied to both everyday activities and to deep religious thought, such as to discussions on how the universe was created.

Al-Kindi must have been fascinated by Aristotle, as he again and again referred to the Greek philosopher's views in his own writings. Just as the work of Socrates affected the work of his student Plato, the work of Aristotle affected the work of al-Kindi. In a way, al-Kindi served as an extension of the great Greek scholars, even though he did not directly study with them and he came from an entirely different background. Aristotle died around 322 BC, long before al-Kindi's birth. Similarly, Euclid influenced al-Kindi, even though he lived around the fourth century BC.

EUCLID

A Greek mathematician who studied under Plato, Euclid taught geometry and founded a school for mathematics. To this day, much of our knowledge about plane geometry, proportions, properties of numbers, magnitudes, and volume comes from Euclid's early teachings. Many of these were included in his book *The Elements*, which Harun al-Rashid so earnestly wanted to have translated into the Arabic language.

Harun al-Rashid and his son al-Mamun knew that their society would benefit if basic skills in math, science, and the liberal arts could be imparted to their people. Profitable business dealings and stable architecture, for example, rely upon these studies. It is no wonder, then, that al-Mamun chose the best and the brightest for his House of Wisdom. The most famous scientists and philosophers within the House of Wisdom were Muhammad ibn Musa al-Khwarizmi (ca. 790–840), the Banu Musa brothers, and al-Kindi.

This is a page from a twelfth-century Arabic translation of *The Elements*, a geometry text by Greek mathematician Euclid *(inset)*, who is known as the father of geometry. Written around 300 BC, *Elements* was for centuries required reading for university students and it remains a primary foundation for modern textbooks on geometry. More than 1,000 editions of the book have been published.

نفصل مر هز سطر طرط مساوی لضعف اب ح وبنی هج مساوی
لمربع اج فاج لقوی علی هم وهو باب ح مجمو عبر مح موسط وضعف
اب و بج موسط وسطح هر مساوی لمربع اب ح مجمو عبر ق سطح
طر مساوی لضعف اب و بج فکل واحد مر د درج منطو ؟
القوه و بازدره فی الطو ومربعا بح مجمو عبر بابن ضعف اب
ع بج فسطح هر بابن سطح زط ودد بابن دح و الطو ونطق
هما فی القوه وزدره فی القوه فقط منطقان
مشترکان ورح اصم وده منطق وسطح هم
اصم والحط القوی علیه اصم وهو اج فاج
اصم فلیدع المنصل

بوسط الکم موسطا ودکل م ارد نا ان نبین
المنفصل لا خط واصر فقط حتی
مثل ان المنفصل خطاب
حد هما قبل الاتصال فا ذل
د را ج جب برها نداه
ینصل به خط بد و را ده مربعی
اج و بج مثل را ده مربع ادد

محو ین

AL-KHWARIZMI

Born in Baghdad around AD 780, al-Khwarizmi is believed by some historians to have been raised as a Zoroastrian. The religion of Zoroastrianism preceded Islam and was founded in the sixth century BC. Followers believed in the prophet Zoroaster and worshipped a god called Ahura Mazda, who stood for the power of good over evil. Astrology formed a part of Zoroastrian beliefs, and al-Khwarizmi remained interested in this area even when he converted to Islam as an adult. In early history, people often linked astrology and astronomy and viewed them as equally valid disciplines.

At the House of Wisdom, al-Khwarizmi worked on translating Greek texts, primarily on algebra and astronomy, into Arabic. To indicate how important his work was, the word "algebra" basically was invented by al-Khwarizmi. In his algebra book, he sought to educate people on all the math skills they would need for daily life and work. He wrote that he desired to impart "what is easiest and most useful in arithmetic, such as men constantly require in cases of inheritance, legacies, partition, lawsuits, and trade, and in all their dealings with one another, or where the measuring of lands, the digging of canals, geometrical computations, and other objects of various sorts are concerned," he wrote in his book *The Compendius Book of Calculation* (*Hisab al-Jabr w'al-Muqabala*). The phrase "al-jabr," meaning in this case "completion," later evolved into the word "algebra." He then went on to define basic concepts about algebra, many of which mathematicians still recognize today.

For astronomy, al-Khwarizmi added to existing knowledge about the stars and planets, much of which came from Indian texts. Al-Khwarizmi studied calendars; the positions of the sun, moon, and the planets; spherical astronomy; astrology; eclipses; and math tables that calculated approximate distances between space objects. In addition to astronomy and algebra, al-Khwarizmi also studied geography. He wrote a paper that was later used for decades in the creation of world maps.

THE BANU MUSA BROTHERS

The Banu Musa brothers were actually three brothers who all worked at the House of Wisdom. They were Jafar Muhammad ibn Musa ibn Shakir (ca. 800–873), Ahmad ibn Musa ibn Shakir (ca. 805–873), and al-Hasan ibn Musa ibn Shakir (ca. 810–873). Their father was a reformed thief named Musa. Not much is known about them individually, except that they lived and worked at around the same time as al-Kindi. "Banu Musa" means "sons of Musa."

Like al-Khwarizmi, the brothers covered many disciplines. They wrote about geometry, astronomy, math, and mechanics. Perhaps their most famous work, credited to them collectively, was *The Book of the Measurement of Plane and Spherical Figures (Kitab Marifat Masakhat al-Ashkal)*. It was later translated into Latin and became the standard by which many readers measured circles, spheres, and cylinders in school and for business purposes. They also contributed important information to the fields of geometry and astronomy. For the latter, they measured the duration of the year and determined that it lasted 365 days and 6 hours, a remarkable finding considering that they did not have the benefit of good telescopes or observation of the earth from space, as scientists do today.

Although the brothers lay claim to many important findings, they are mostly known as al-Kindi's rivals. This competitiveness grew over time and came to a head when the House of Wisdom underwent changes because of political transitions.

NEW LEADERSHIP

When al-Mamun died in 833, he was succeeded by one of his brothers, al-Mutasim, who only lived nine more years. In 842, al-Wathiq came to power. He, in turn, did not live for very long after he began ruling. In 847, al-Wathiq was succeeded by al-Mutawakkil (821–861). During the leadership of al-Wathiq and al-Mutawakkil, a shake-up began to occur in the House of Wisdom. Members of the house started to

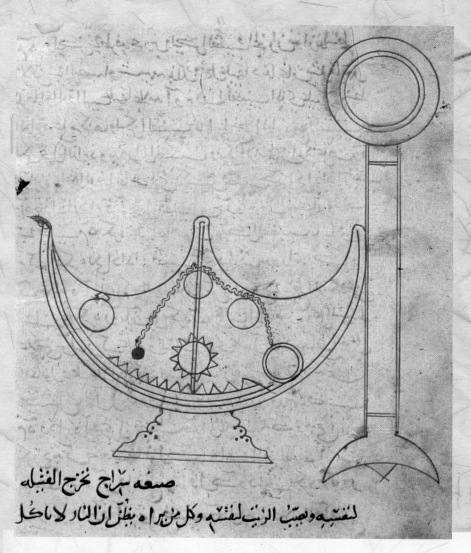

Ahmad ibn Musa ibn Shakir, one of the Banu Musa brothers, included this drawing of a self-trimming lamp in his treatise on mechanical devices. The Banu Musa brothers were among the most powerful and revered scholars in the House of Wisdom. Like their peers, they studied and wrote about a wide range of subjects.

Built during the reign of al-Mutawakkil, the Great Mosque is the largest mosque in the world. Its minaret, or tower, which is shown here, is 180 feet (55 m) high. It is located in Samarra, Iraq.

compete with each other for political favors.

It was well known that the Banu Musa brothers were jealous over al-Kindi's personal library, which he had built up over many years, and his high status within the House of Wisdom. The library was called al-Kindiyah, and it contained several valuable texts. According to some later written histories, the brothers schemed against al-Kindi and conspired with al-Mutawakkil to try to get al-Kindi to leave the House of Wisdom. As a result, according to these histories, al-Kindi was dismissed from the house. The al-Kindiyah library was also confiscated.

Over time, al-Kindi's library was restored to him. According to some historians, this occurred through the help of a friend who had to resort to subtle extortion to regain the valuable collection. Once again, al-Kindi was allowed to work at the House of Wisdom. However, he lost many privileges within the court at that time, and his reputation was sullied. How and why this occurred remains a mystery. It is only documented that al-Kindi died about 866, somewhat disgraced from his once spotless image. Al-Kindi loved solitude. His death is said to have been very quiet in terms of public reaction. It is likely that his competitors had a hand in affecting his reputation and his later legacy. Thankfully, many of al-Kindi's works have since resurfaced. It is now known just how much he really did contribute to philosophy, alchemy, physics, medicine, cryptanalysis, calligraphy, math, music, geography, astronomy, and seemingly countless other subjects.

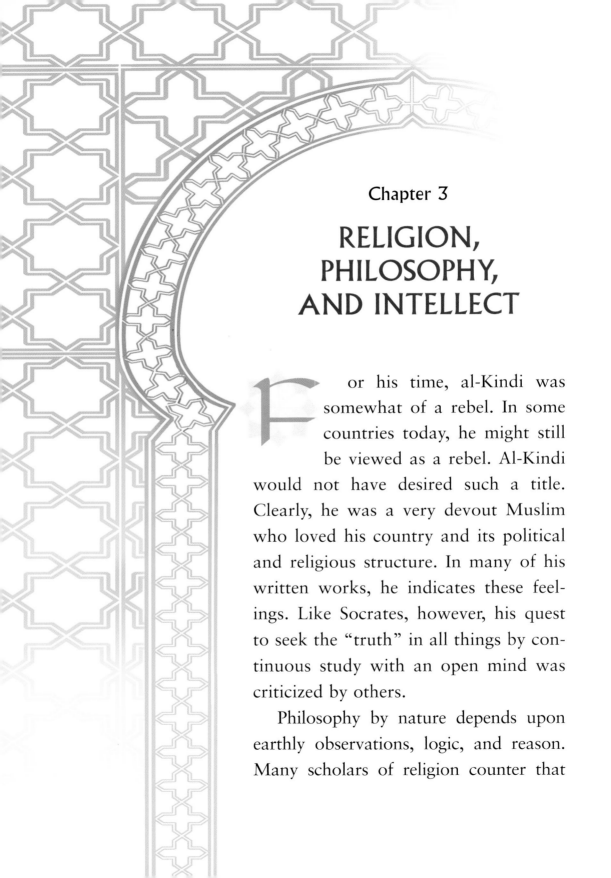

Chapter 3

RELIGION, PHILOSOPHY, AND INTELLECT

For his time, al-Kindi was somewhat of a rebel. In some countries today, he might still be viewed as a rebel. Al-Kindi would not have desired such a title. Clearly, he was a very devout Muslim who loved his country and its political and religious structure. In many of his written works, he indicates these feelings. Like Socrates, however, his quest to seek the "truth" in all things by continuous study with an open mind was criticized by others.

Philosophy by nature depends upon earthly observations, logic, and reason. Many scholars of religion counter that revelation and faith are necessary for religious beliefs and theories. Due in part to these differences, many conservative people of the Islamic faith held philosophers like al-Kindi in very low esteem. In fact, philosophers often were attacked, both verbally and physically, because they were considered to be heretics. During his lifetime, al-Kindi was told that "acquisition of the knowledge of the reality of things is atheism," as recorded in *A History of Muslim Philosophy*. Defending himself, al-Kindi said of such accusers, "They disputed with good men in defense of the untrue position which they had founded and occupied without any merit only to gain power and to trade with religion."

Socrates was clearly a philosophical role model for al-Kindi. He is considered to be one of the pillars of Western philosophy even though there is no evidence of his ever writing down his views.

A HARMONIOUS ACCORD

Al-Kindi was a talented wordsmith. He played with the meanings of words to achieve desired definitions. Shakespeare also did this in his writings, and the playwright even invented some words that still are in the English language today. In al-Kindi's paper *On the Definitions of Things and Their Descriptions* (*Risalah fi Huded al-Ashya'wa Rusumiha*), the Arab scholar's views about philosophy and religion are clarified with the clever use of language.

For example, he defined philosophy in six ways. First he pointed out the Greek roots of the word. *Philo* means "friend," and *sophia* means "wisdom," so philosophy is the love of wisdom. He then said philosophy enabled humans to copy divine excellence as much as is possible. He added that philosophy touches upon the meaning of death and the soul. It is, according to al-Kindi, the "science of sciences" and the "wisdom of wisdoms," which allows man to know himself. He also explained that philosophy is the study of essence and causes, in as much as humans are capable of learning about them.

The last provision is essential to understanding al-Kindi because no matter how much he supported philosophy and science, he always made clear that these pursuits could never equal the ultimate truth, which he believed was God. Whether it was from personal beliefs or governmental pressure, al-Kindi always made sure that a reverence to God superceded anything that he said or did.

Unlike some of today's fundamentalist leaders, al-Kindi believed that a harmonious accord could be found between religion and philosophy, which in his case could also refer to

STUDIES IN ISLAMIC PHILOSOPHY AND SCIENCE

Published under the auspices of
the Society for the Study of Islamic Philosophy and Science

AL-KINDI'S METAPHYSICS

A Translation of
Ya'qūb ibn Isḥāq al-Kindī's Treatise
"ON FIRST PHILOSOPHY"
(fī al-Falsafah al-Ūlā)

with Introduction and Commentary by

Alfred L. Ivry

---

p. 97   *IN THE NAME OF GOD THE MERCIFUL*
THE COMPASSIONATE
MY SUCCESS IS IN GOD ALONE

Al-Kindī's Book, for al-Mu'taṣim Billāh

On First Philosophy

5 /May God grant you long life, O son[1] of the highest of princes and of the (strongest) bonds of bliss; of those who, whoever holds fast to their guidance is happy in the abode of this life and the abode of eternity; and may He adorn you with all the accoutrements of virtue and cleanse you from all the dirtiness of vice.

Indeed, the human art which is highest in degree and most noble in rank is the art of philosophy, the definition of which is knowledge of the true nature of things, insofar as is possible for man. The aim of the philosopher is, as regards his knowl-

10 edge, /to attain the truth, and as regards his action, to act truthfully; not that the activity is endless, for we abstain and the activity ceases, once we have reached[2] the truth.

We do not find the truth we are seeking without finding a cause; the cause of the existence and continuance of everything is the True One, in that each thing which has being has truth. The True One exists necessarily, and therefore[3] beings exist.

[1]Ms. يابن , as AH. AR يا ابن .

[2]AR يلقنا . Ms. اتيها يلقنا with a line through يلقنا .

[3]Ms. اذا . AR إذن .

55

These pages are from a twentieth-century English language translation of al-Kindi's *On First Philosophy*. His work developing a vocabulary for Arab for Arab philosophical thought laid the groundwork for later, more recognized, Muslim philosophers.

the pursuit of science and logic. He said that theology was a part of philosophy, and that philosophy and the revelations of God to Muhammad are in agreement with each other. He then added that the pursuit of theology is supported by logic, meaning that, in his view, it was natural for people to question the meaning of life and creation, and to conclude that a supreme creator was responsible for everything in existence.

AN ARGUMENT FOR GOD

Al-Kindi wrote many texts about God and creation, but two stand out because they focus primarily on these particular subjects. The treatises are *On First Philosophy* (*Fi al-Flasefa al-Usa*) and *On the Unity of God and the Finitude of the Body of the Universe* (*Ali ibn Jahm fi Wahdaniyat Alla wa Tanahi Jirm al-Alam*). In these texts, al-Kindi reveals that he was influenced by some of Aristotle's writings but that he has come to his own unique conclusions rooted in Islamic thought. One conclusion hinged upon his ability to develop several "proofs" for God's existence.

There were five proofs in total. The first stated that the universe must have been created because it is a finite body that has motion, not unlike humans, plants, and animals, all of which seem to have a period of creation followed by an observed end. Anything that is created must have a creator, according to al-Kindi, so there must be a God.

For the second proof, al-Kindi stated that since creation exists as a unified whole, the creator himself must exist as a single force that is indivisible. Here he somewhat deviated from certain Christians and Greek scholars who theorized that holy power could be divided into three parts. Christian churches described God as a holy trinity. Prior Greek philosophers had also written about how such a sacred being must exist in three forms.

Al-Kindi's third proof argues that a created thing cannot be the cause of itself. If it were, it would have existed before its creation, which is illogical. Here, as in all of the other proofs, al-Kindi shows how his mind works like that of a scientist. The subject may have been spiritual in nature, but his arguments were founded upon science-inspired logic and reason. This way of thinking, of basing one finding on a prior conclusion, is still common in science today.

For his fourth proof, al-Kindi said that just as humans know souls exist, it is also possible to know that God exists. He believed that the wisdom in what he thought was a person's soul reflected upon the "wise administration" of God in the material world. The final proof again reveals this optimism because al-Kindi said that the wonders of all creation could not be "purposeless and accidental" because they simply are too profound and great. He believed that everyone could strive for such perfection and that people are inherently good. This love of life, his fellow man, and of creation shines through many of al-Kindi's works.

CREATIO EX NIHILO

One of the most common phrases associated with al-Kindi's philosophy is *creatio ex nihilo*. This is a Latin phrase that means "creation out of nothing." Al-Kindi believed that God was the only creator of the universe and that he created it out of nothing, meaning that nothing else existed before God's creation. The reason this idea is so tied to al-Kindi is that it distinguished his views and those of the Arabs from the theories of the Greeks.

Al-Kindi often agreed with Aristotle, but he disagreed when it came to creation. Aristotle viewed God not as a creator, but as a force that turned something with potential into reality. Aristotle, who often studied astronomy, saw that the planets and stars appeared to be finite objects. In other words, they were not eternal and infinite. If the creation was not infinite, then the creator may not be either. It is a sign of al-Kindi's open-mindedness that he was able to strongly challenge Aristotle's views on this point, while still respecting other theories of Aristotle's.

What is interesting is that al-Kindi did not rely upon religious dogma to make his argument. He remained ever the scientist. He said that there were four possibilities as to how

During al-Kindi's time and for centuries to follow, Muslim scholars were studying and debating the works of the ancient Greek philosophers who were largely forgotten in Europe. Aristotle, portrayed instructing students using an astrolabe in this thirteenth-century illustration, was a particular favorite of the Muslims.

the universe could have been created. The first possibility is that a thing is nonexistent and that its creator is nonexistent. To believe that, one would have to believe that nothing exists. Moving on, his second possibility is that a thing is nonexistent but its creator is existent. This, too, is impossible, since the creator is revealed in the creation. His third suggestion, that a thing could be existent but could have no creator also was ruled out as illogical, as was his fourth possibility that a thing could be existent along with its creator. If both existed simultaneously, where was the instance of creation? To al-Kindi, the matter was purely logical. God exists, he said. According to al-Kindi, God created the world because it made perfect rational sense to someone who saw the world as a great and glorious place.

THE SOUL

Continuing al-Kindi's optimism is his argument that humans can achieve excellence, nobility, and happiness, all of a divine nature. In a way, this mirrors the Christian belief that man was created in God's image, but al-Kindi did not put so much focus on the literal meaning of that belief. Instead, he emphasized the divine qualities of the soul. As quoted in *Al-Kindi's Philosophical Treatises* (*Rasa'il al-Kindi al-Falsafiya*), the edition of al-Kindi's works by M. A. Abu Ridah, al-Kindi described the soul as

> . . . simple, and of a perfect nature. Its essence derives from the essence of the Creator, just as sunshine is derived from the sun. It has been explained that the soul is separate from the body and different from it, and that its essence is divine and spiritual in view of the excellence of its nature and its aversion to the passion and irascibility that blight the body.

While al-Kindi believed in the oneness of God, he thought that the human soul could be divided into three parts and that the soul in its entirety was immortal. Plato first proposed the division of the soul into parts. One part is said to be intellectual; another is passionate; and a third is concupiscent, or desirous. Plato compared the intellectual part to a charioteer, with the other two helping to drive the chariot.

Al-Kindi did not have much good to say about passion and desire. He felt that they moved man to commit great sins. He observed that people who retained their calm sense of reason had more control and got into less trouble. As an artistic person, however, al-Kindi did support what he called the "imaginative faculty." It is with this that he shows himself as a unique and groundbreaking philosopher.

No other known Muslim writer and teacher before al-Kindi had ever stated that personal visions associated with imagination and dreams were natural and not the product of some kind of supernatural phenomena. During his time, many people believed that such thoughts somehow existed outside of the person. Al-Kindi stopped short of challenging the visions of the Prophet, however, and instead said that Muhammad's visions represented a truth that no mere mortal could dream up. He did believe that every person was capable of knowing the same truth through the use of his or her imaginative faculties, which seemed to represent his notion of the soul's purity.

اول قدرته اول عظمته حيران قلدرقاموسنك صدق
ارتدى يقين لرى درست اولدى عباس نن مرد اس دُ اُ جُخُ

حضرت عباس

اهل و عيالى طوارن مالى الدى بله يورودى جُون علّى
المرتضى عباس جماعت بله قزلر اُروُدى خُى اُيوزندن

Such a theory is again very optimistic because it brings a certain power back to the people. Truth can be found from within, and not just on the orders of another person. Many religions, including Hinduism and Christianity, came to embrace this view as well. It puts the emphasis back on the individual. In a way, al-Kindi was more democratic in his thinking than many Western religious and political leaders are today. The belief also indicates how much importance al-Kindi placed on the arts. If the imaginative faculties were divine, then their material creations must reflect this divinity. Music and art, therefore, were thought to have power and healing properties. One legend about al-Kindi is that he once healed a neighbor's child from a severe illness simply by playing music for the youngster.

Entitled *The Miracle of the Bees*, this sixteenth-century illustration from Mustafa Darir's *The Life of the Prophet (Sayir-e-Nabi)* was added two centuries after Darir wrote the manuscript. The manuscript documents key events in Muhammad's career as prophet, including visits from the angel Gabriel.

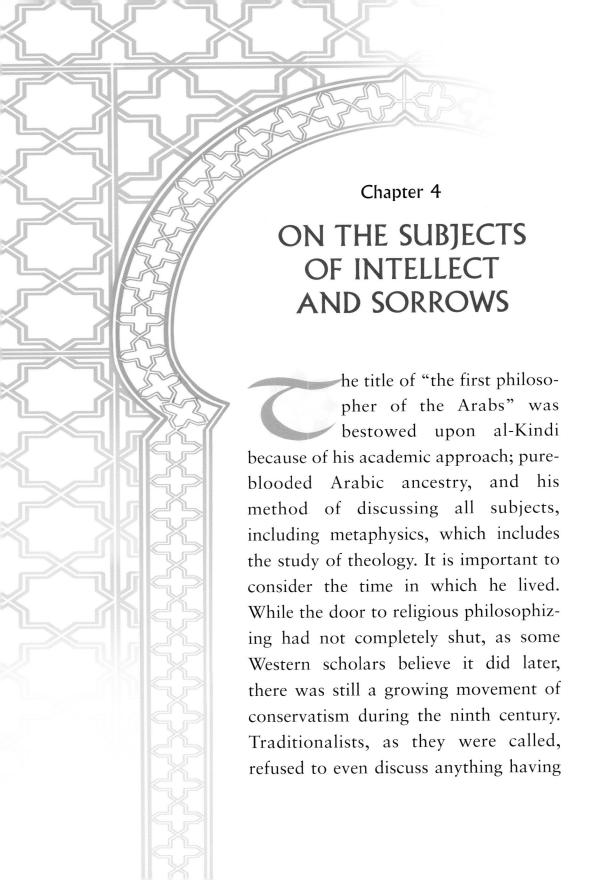

Chapter 4

ON THE SUBJECTS OF INTELLECT AND SORROWS

The title of "the first philosopher of the Arabs" was bestowed upon al-Kindi because of his academic approach; pure-blooded Arabic ancestry, and his method of discussing all subjects, including metaphysics, which includes the study of theology. It is important to consider the time in which he lived. While the door to religious philosophizing had not completely shut, as some Western scholars believe it did later, there was still a growing movement of conservatism during the ninth century. Traditionalists, as they were called, refused to even discuss anything having to do with God. The subject was deemed heretical and off-limits. For example, when one famous traditionalist, Ahmad ibn Hanbal (780–855), was asked a question about the Qur'an, he refused to answer. He later said that the Qur'an was the word of God and then suggested that this was not up for discussion.

Another group, called the Mutazilites, also existed during al-Kindi's time. According to many historians, these men, while devoutly religious, held the more liberal view that issues concerning God, creation, and related subjects were open to discussion and

Like the other portraits of al-Kindi in this book, this is a speculative depiction of the father of Arab philosophy. There is no recorded evidence of what he actually looked like.

debate. Al-Kindi did not always agree with the Mutazilites, but he did adhere to their view that theology could and should be discussed, even among the devout. Al-Kindi once wrote that he followed "the way of the logicians," which was likely in reference to the Mutazilites. The Mutazilites opened theology to discussion, which placed an emphasis

This is a manuscript page from al-Kindi's *Epistle on the Doctrine About the Soul Summarized from the Book of Aristotle and Plato and the Rest of the Philosophers*. In it, he outlines and discusses Aristotle's views on intellect, and adds his original philosophy about a soul-intellect connection.

on logic, or reasoning, as opposed to discourse relying solely on faith-based principles.

What is remarkable for readers of al-Kindi today is his consistency. Whether the subject was God or science, he used the same studied, logical methods of discussion. Clearly, he made every effort to quell any personal prejudices in an effort to find what he called the truth. The truth for al-Kindi, while rooted in God, could emerge from any source, even the maligned "foreign sciences" (scholarly works and theories from outside areas, such as Greece and India). Few people before or after al-Kindi managed to uphold such high, consistent standards of scholarship. He applied this same reasoning to philosophical teachings about intellect, knowledge, and sorrows.

INTELLECT

Before al-Kindi, Aristotle had written about the nature of intellect, which he divided into three kinds. Al-Kindi reinterpreted Aristotle's theory and added a fourth kind. It is unclear whether he misread Aristotle's original work or if he chose to adapt it for his Arabic readers. In any case, al-Kindi's theory remains uniquely his own.

The first kind of intellect, according to al-Kindi, is the intellect that is always in action. It is the part of us that continuously perceives what is going on around us, such as sounds, smells, tangible things, other people, and so on. His second kind of intellect is one that is "potentially in the soul." This refers to someone's ability to act, a capacity that is not necessarily realized. For example, an artist has the ability to draw even before he realizes this talent on paper. The third intellect serves as a transition from the second to the fourth, which is when the person actually uses his or her mental capabilities to do something, such as drawing or writing. In this fourth stage, the mind's potential is realized into something concrete and tangible.

Note that al-Kindi creates a link between a person's intellect and his or her soul. He believed that life is sacred and not just a means to a heavenly afterlife, although that was important to him. He also believed that a person's actions were important and could influence the actions of others. These views again went against the principles of the traditionalists because al-Kindi emphasized individuals and their connection with God through what he called the "soul," instead of emphasizing submission and group thought. However, he made very clear that the main goal of his philosophy was to know God, whom Muslims call Allah. Al-Kindi equated God with truth.

KNOWLEDGE

Al-Kindi believed that all humans perceive the world in two ways, through the senses and through knowledge via

This thirteenth-century illustration depicting a public library in Hulwan (Baghdad) is from the *Maqamat* (The Assemblies) by al-Hariri. Successive Muslim caliphs supported institutions such as libraries and schools during the age of the Muslim Empire. Mosques also played a significant role in the spread of knowledge in the empire.

the aforementioned intellects. He distinguished between the material world and the world that a human can create in his or her mind through dreams or the imagination. Al-Kindi then divided what we perceive into two categories. The first category consists of material objects, or what he called particulars. He called the second category universals, referring to the world of dreams and imagination.

Al-Kindi placed more value on universals and intellectual knowledge than on particulars. He believed that they were superior because they allow an individual to grasp tough, complex issues and problems that everyday experience may not resolve. For example, he often liked to use the so-called law of noncontradiction to turn metaphysical problems into questions of logic.

The law of noncontradiction can be stated as the math equation "either A or B, not A, therefore B." To put this into practice, al-Kindi said things like, "If the universe is a body then either it is infinite in quantity or is quantitatively finite. The universe cannot be quantitatively infinite. Therefore, the universe is quantitatively finite," as quoted by Mashhad Al-Allaf. He then concluded that the universe is not eternal, but instead had a distinct beginning and so will have a distinct end.

Different Approaches for Different Subjects

Although al-Kindi studied many subjects, he believed that each one required its own unique method of study. According to Mashhad Al-Allaf, he wrote:

We ought, however, to aim at what is required for each pursuit, and not pursue probability in the science of mathematics, nor sensation or exemplification in the science of the metaphysical; nor conceptual generalization in the principles of the science of the physical; nor demonstration in rhetoric, nor demonstration in the principles of demonstration. Surely if we observe these conditions the pursuits which are intended will become easy for us but if we disobey this, we will miss the objectives of our pursuits, and the perception of our intended objects will become difficult.

His method must have worked. Al-Kindi was able to analyze information about linguistics, physics, math, and metaphysics, all seemingly at the same time. He organized his mind and his methods to accommodate the different fields of study. In doing so, he actually helped to define these subjects. Today, we take it for granted that schools teach such subjects as math and languages separately. Those separations came from centuries of findings, many of which were derived from al-Kindi's works.

Emperor Nero ruled Rome between AD 54 and AD 68. His reign was marked by cruelty and conspiracy. He persecuted Christians, whom he blamed for a devastating fire in Rome.

ON THE MEANS TO DRIVE AWAY SORROWS

Al-Kindi also taught and wrote on the subject of ethics, which is a philosophical discipline concerning morality and obligation. Only one of his works on ethics survives in a complete form today. It is called *On the Means to Drive Away Sorrows* (*Fi al-Hila Li-Daf al-Ahzan*). Here, without fear of reprisal from the traditionalists or the government, al-Kindi's own optimistic and clever voice shines through.

He believed that sorrow results from three things: the desire for what is unattainable or difficult to get; anticipating these things that a person would like to own; and then what happens to us when these things are either lost or never obtained. "Things" in this case could refer to material objects or to people. For example, a student could desire a new bicycle or a new relationship with someone. When the object or person becomes lost or is unattainable in the first place, disappointment can result.

To avoid sorrow, al-Kindi advises that we should only place value on things that really matter to us. We should strive to curb our passions in order to maintain what he called a spiritual equilibrium. He places far more value on people, ideas, and religion than he does on material wealth. To illustrate the points, he tells an old tale about the Roman emperor Nero (AD 37–68).

Nero coveted a fancy canopy, or tent, to shelter him. Given the importance of such tents in Arab culture at the time, it would be like a mansion today. When Nero expressed his desire for the object, a philosopher said, "If you should ever lose this canopy, you will never be able to replace it. Great will be your sorrow, for your poverty in front of the impossible will be laid bare." Nero ignored the advice and went to great pains to have the canopy shipped to him by boat. The boat sank and it is said that Nero became so depressed that he died of sorrow. The moral of al-Kindi's story is that we should try to overcome our desire for external possessions.

In yet another lesson, al-Kindi shares a story about the Greek leader Alexander the Great (356–323 BC). Shortly before Alexander died, al-Kindi said that he wrote a letter to his mother telling her that should he ever die, she should hold a big party and invite only people who had

Entitled *Mourning for Iskander*, this sixteenth-century miniature portrays a funeral procession for Alexander the Great, who was known as Iskander among Arabs. Alexander the Great ruled over Arabian territories from 334 BC until his death in 323 BC.

not experienced grief and sorrow. When Alexander died, his mother sent out invitations with the provision Alexander had mentioned. No one showed up. She then learned that everyone experiences grief and sorrow at some point in their lives. That was the lesson Alexander meant to teach her, and it is the one that al-Kindi shared with his readers.

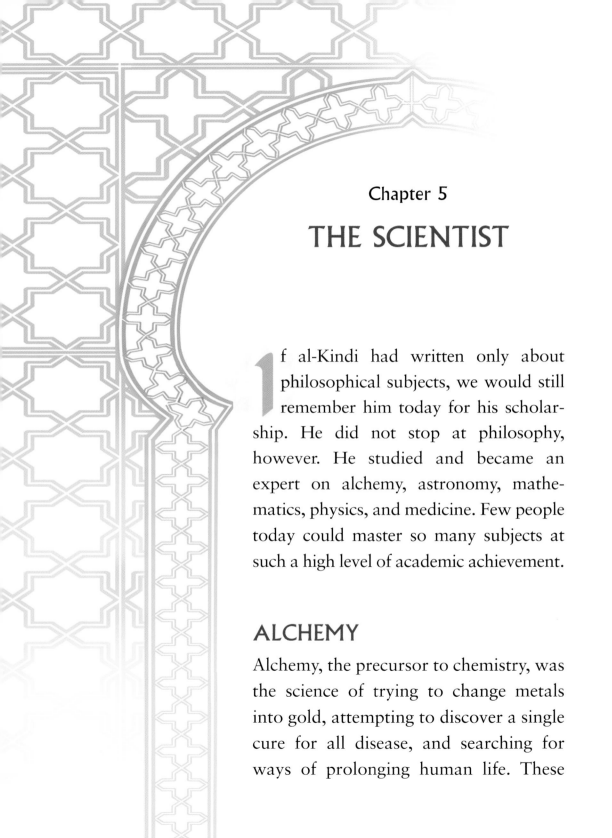

Chapter 5

THE SCIENTIST

I f al-Kindi had written only about philosophical subjects, we would still remember him today for his scholarship. He did not stop at philosophy, however. He studied and became an expert on alchemy, astronomy, mathematics, physics, and medicine. Few people today could master so many subjects at such a high level of academic achievement.

ALCHEMY

Alchemy, the precursor to chemistry, was the science of trying to change metals into gold, attempting to discover a single cure for all disease, and searching for ways of prolonging human life. These seemingly unrelated subjects are grouped together under the term "alchemy," a field that no longer really exists today because so many of its goals have been proven impossible by scientists or are not yet feasible given today's technologies.

Al-Kindi was far ahead of his time in seeing the problems with alchemy. He wrote at least two papers on the subject, "Warning Against the Deceptions of the Alchemists," (*I-Tanbih ala al-Khida al-Kimiya'in*) and "Refutation of the Claim of Those Who Claim the Artificial Fabrication of Gold and Silver." Hard as it is to believe today, people in the ancient world, including Cleopatra (69–30 BC) and the scientists in her court, believed that people could transform base metals, like iron, into gold. The desire was understandable, given the value that gold and silver had then and still do today. From his scientific studies, al-Kindi knew such a goal was impossible.

ASTRONOMY

Al-Kindi wrote at least twenty-three texts on astronomy, and he mentions the movement of stars and planets in his other works, such as those on metaphysics. In his writings, he tackled such issues as the motion of the moon, the projection of sun rays, astrology, the length of days, retrograde motion, stellar rays, the sun, the origin of rain, and other weather-related issues. At the time, weather studies were often linked to astronomy.

Early Astronomy

The Arabs helped to found the field of astronomy, much as we know it today. Their incentive was very different, however, from what drives most astronomers in the Western world. Instead of just being curious about the stars and planets, they used the movement of celestial bodies to determine fasting periods for the holy month of Ramadan and other important religious events. To create a more accurate system of measurement, Arab scientists improved upon the astrolabe, a compact instrument that astronomers used to determine the positions of stars. Later a tool called the sextant replaced it.

Using astrolabes, scientists like al-Kindi wrote down data that was inserted into astronomical charts and tables. Ruling bodies supported such work, especially because of its religious importance, so they paid to build observatories. Two of the most famous ones in the Middle Ages were at Palmyra and Maragha. At first, these measurements were rather crude and inaccurate. As time went on, however, knowledge passed down from various scientists led to fairly accurate findings on the length of degrees, longitude and latitude, and the relative speeds of light and sound. Arab astronomers even figured out that Earth rotates on its own axis, a theory that was not proven until 600 years later.

MATH

Al-Kindi wrote numerous books and papers on arithmetic, geometry, and spherics, or the study of spheres, which includes analysis of the shape of Earth. The titles of these books indicate how well-versed al-Kindi was on math theories

Muslim scholars greatly advanced human knowledge of astronomy during the period of the European Middle Ages. They refined astronomical instruments and existing theories, and they made new discoveries that were useful in developing more accurate calendars and maps. This sixteenth-century illustration from *Shahinshahnama* (Book of the King of Kings) portrays astronomers working in an armillary sphere, a type of observatory.

from around the world. For example he wrote *On the Use of Indian Numerals (Isti'malal' Hisab al' Hindi)*, and then followed it up with *On Explanation of the Numbers Mentioned by Plato in his Politics (L-Ibanah 'an al A'dad Allet Dhakarah Flatun fi 'l-Sisayah)*. He also came up with his own theories. Some educators and historians today believe that al-Kindi's work laid down the foundation for modern arithmetic, but others believe that he was outdone by al-Khwarizmi, his colleague in the House of Wisdom.

What is clear is that mathematics as we know it today was largely shaped by the efforts of al-Kindi, al-Khwarizmi, and other Arab and Muslim scholars. The Arabs clarified the concept of zero, which led to entirely new theories about math. They also developed trigonometry, and al-Khwarizmi founded the study of algebra. Both he and al-Kindi were involved in this important work primarily for practical purposes. They desired better, more efficient ways of measuring plots of land. They were following the Qur'an, which contains instructions about land inheritance. Calculations derived from algebra and

Al-Khwarizmi's book of algebra, *Kitab al-Jabr wal-Muqabala*, is one of the most influential products of the Muslim Empire. The book's title literally means "the compendious book on calculation by completion and balancing." He is widely acknowledged as the inventor of the mathematical field of algebra, the name of which is derived from the title of his book. His name is itself the source for "algorithm," another branch of mathematics.

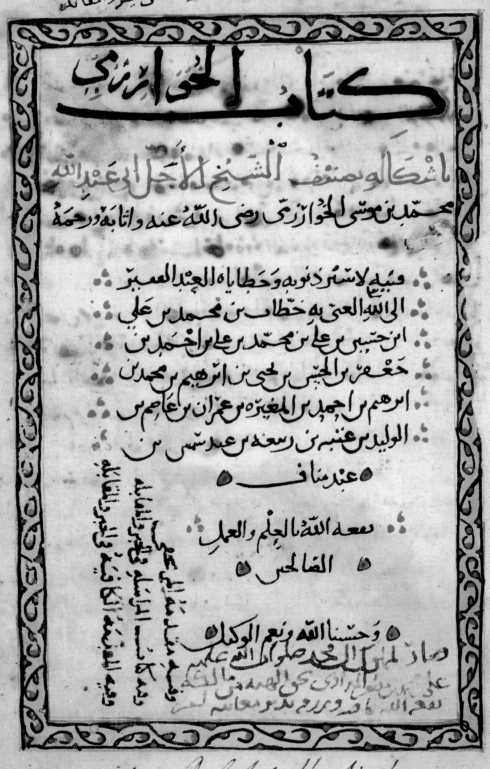

كتاب الجبر والمقابلة

اشكاله وصنف الشيخ الاجل ابو عبد الله
محمد بن موسى الخوارزمي رضى الله عنه واثابه ورحمه

وبيع لاستردنوبه وخطاياه العبد المعير
الى الله العنى به خطاب بن محمد بن علي
ابن حبيب بن علي بن محمد بن علي بن احمد بن
جعفر بن الحبيب بن يحيى بن ابراهيم بن محمد بن
ابرهم بن احمد بن المغيره بن عمران بن عاصم بن
الوليد بن عنبر بن رسعد بن عبد شمس بن
عبد مناف

نفعه الله بالعلم والعمل
الصالح

وحسبنا الله ونعم الوكيل
صاد لمالك المحمد صلوات الله عليه
على خير بقول المرادى حتى الهمه من الفقه
لفقر الله ... وررحم بذره معاشه ...

geometry improved their ability to measure land, but these fields of study have had numerous other applications since then, ranging from business to architecture to all forms of design.

PHYSICS

Physics is the science of matter, energy, and their interactions. Few people in the ancient world thought much about physics, except in terms of metaphysics, which is a division of philosophy that is concerned with the reality of being, God, creation, and related issues. Here again, al-Kindi stands apart from his contemporaries because he studied matter, motion, and time, the same subjects that challenged great scientists like Albert Einstein (1879–1955) many hundreds of years later.

Following al-Kindi's belief that the universe is finite, the Arab scientist believed that motion and time also are finite. In other words, he predicted that the motion and time connected to any object or event had a definite beginning and end. They therefore could be measured. While tools to make accurate measurements did not even exist in the ninth century, al-Kindi foresaw what would occur centuries later in science, when better clocks and other methods of measurement would be invented. His notion that scientists could quantify most things on earth extended to his highly influential work on medicine.

MEDICINE

No evidence exists that al-Kindi practiced as a physician, but it is possible, given the anecdote about how he supposedly cured a neighbor's son with music. He also wrote many books on the subject of medicine. Some of these works are outdated now, but not necessarily due to faults on the part of al-Kindi. He was limited mostly to visual observations of patients and did not have the benefit of microscopes, knowledge of germs, and later findings. He wrote a book on mucus, for example. It was called *On the Fits Resulting from Phlegm and the Cause of Sudden Death (L'-A'rad al-Hadithath min al-Balgham wa 'Illah Mawt al Fuja'ah)*. Anything and everything in his world interested al-Kindi, who had a genuine desire to help his fellow man. In *On the Fits*, he analyzes the behavior of afflicted patients with impressive detail. Likely, this degree of attention led to some cure and comfort for the patients he attempted to help.

Without question, al-Kindi's most important work on medicine was *De Medicinarum Compositarum Gradibus Investigandis Libellus* (The Investigation of the Strength of Compound Medicines). The treatise concerns posology, a branch of medicine that al-Kindi practically invented that deals with the dosages of drugs. (Before al-Kindi, there was little scientific analysis on this issue.) In the book, he describes all sorts of medicines that physicians and other

من كتاب ثاطيغورياس الذى للحكيم قال سمتى وما اختنرت ى كتاب تا طيغورياس
اولا وما جعلته الذى للحكيم قال خنين ان ا كتاب تا طيغورياس فلا انه ابتدأ
هذا الحلو اما ا ما الذى للحكيم فلا انه ليس عندكم وجود انى هذا الوقت مما علم به
هذا المعنى المقصود قال سمتى ان ما هنا كما با اخرلواضح لاخرى هذا المعنى
لولا ان وجود ت الكتب الاختياره ى اميل قال ثم كتاب ارفع طسرى هذا المعنى
قال سمتى ومن احوط صر هذا قال خنين انسان من شيعته فيثا غورس قال
سمتى من فيثا غورس هذا اورنان ت قال خنين ان جل كان رسوا المبتدى كذلك
حكمة اليو نائنيه وليس انما هو ى العنا نقبل الكلم كثير وقبل افلا طون ايضا
وعنه اخذ هذا الحلم وليس هذا العن من النظر فقط بل جميع العنون الباقينه
وكذلك اوقليدس ى البو سرو ارسطيدس وبطليمو سى ساير المهندسين م

ابو يوسف يعقوب بن اسمق الكندك

هواول من خرج من المسلمين ى الفلسفه و ساير اجزا يهاو ى الرياضيات وما يتعلق
بها سوى تبحره ى علوم العرب و براعته من الاداب بن النحو والشعرولحكام
النجوم والطب وضروب من الصناعات والمعارف التي تنال بها يجمع معارفها
ى انسان واحد وما فيهم رست كتبه يزيد على كمت كاعذمشى وله راستاذ احمد
بن محد المعتصم وبا سمه على الكثر كتبه واليه كتب جل رسايله ولجوته مسايله
وهواول من احدث هذه الطريقه التى اخذ اما بعده من جام الاسلا مين وان كان
قد تقدمه من ارتفع اسمه و حسنت حاله ى ايام ما منون من الذين كان
طبهم نصارى و نضا يهم كبرى لا مرفيه ع الدم القديم ولا شتها كتبه
ورسايله و تداول الا يدى بها وسخه وجود ها ى كل موضع م استقص نطلب
الكتب واستقى اما منها ع الحاذره ى اشا بها الا البسير الذى ما جديد من تدريب

هذا الكتاب؟

This is a page from *On the Fits Resulting from Phlegm and the Cause of Sudden Death*, al-Kindi's manuscript on mucus. One of Iraq's leading hospitals is named for al-Kindi in recognition of his contributions to medicine.

healers used to cure various ailments at the time. Virtually all of these medicines came from natural botanical sources. That tradition would continue well into the medieval period, with monks and physicians who studied plant medicines, and even to modern times, which have witnessed a revival of interest in natural medicines.

Dosages for such drugs were a guessing game in the ancient world. Today, we take such things for granted. When a person swallows an aspirin, for example, the aspirin comes in a certain size and strength. Medicine in al-Kindi's day was more like what is practiced by Chinese herbalists today. They had to measure out natural ingredients to order for every patient.

Before al-Kindi, another early scientist named Galen (AD 131–201) created a method of distributing drugs based upon degrees of intensity. These degrees relied upon qualities, often abstract, such as "warmth and coldness" and "wetness and dryness." If a drug was considered to be "hot" and the patient needed less "warmth," the pharmacist was to add some other ingredient to make the concoction "colder." The system confused many, with the result that drug dosages were never standardized, that is, until al-Kindi.

Using brilliant deduction, al-Kindi applied math calculations to the prior work on degrees of warmth. He created an easy-to-use table that pharmacists could refer to when creating prescriptions. If a drug was to be neither warm nor cold, then it should have one part warm ingredient and one part

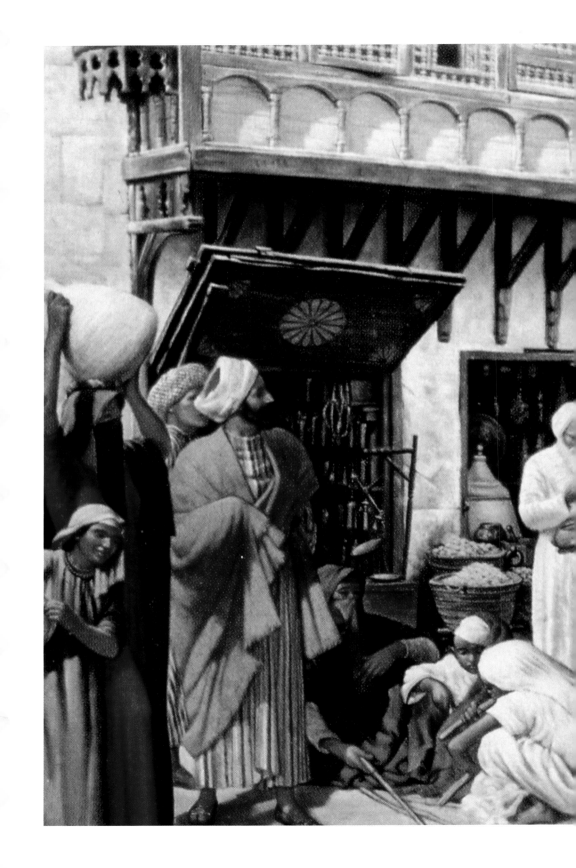

Entitled *The First Apothecary Shop*, this 1952 painting by American Robert A. Thom imagines history's first pharmacy. It was published in *A History of Pharmacy in Pictures*. Set in the Muslim Empire in AD 745, the painting salutes the pioneering role of the Arabs in pharmacology.

cold ingredient, which would cancel out any warmth. If the first degree of warmth was desired, the drug mixture should contain two parts warm to one part cold. For the second degree of warmth, three parts warm were added to one part cold, and so on. By documenting amounts with a formula that anyone could follow, al-Kindi revolutionized medicine. Drugs now could be formulated according to set amounts with the result that all patients would receive standardized dosages.

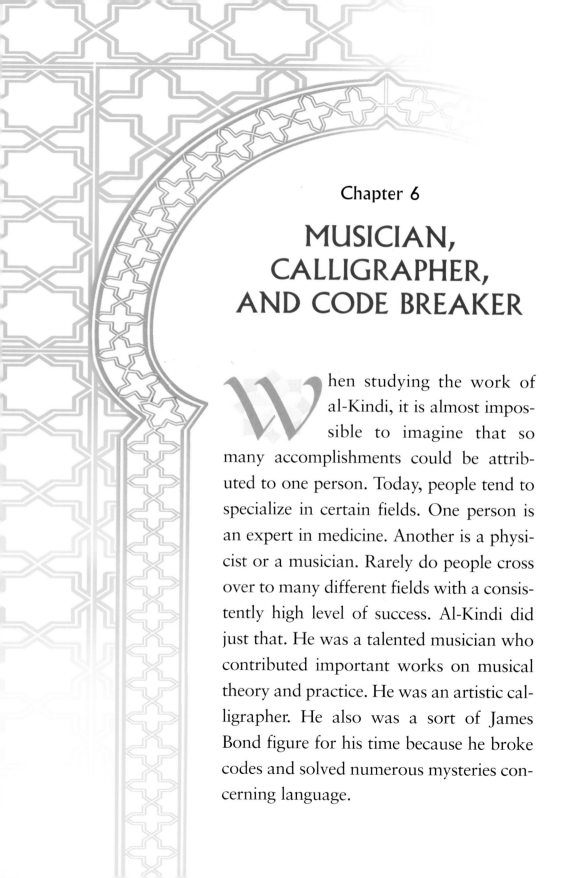

Chapter 6

MUSICIAN, CALLIGRAPHER, AND CODE BREAKER

When studying the work of al-Kindi, it is almost impossible to imagine that so many accomplishments could be attributed to one person. Today, people tend to specialize in certain fields. One person is an expert in medicine. Another is a physicist or a musician. Rarely do people cross over to many different fields with a consistently high level of success. Al-Kindi did just that. He was a talented musician who contributed important works on musical theory and practice. He was an artistic calligrapher. He also was a sort of James Bond figure for his time because he broke codes and solved numerous mysteries concerning language.

This manuscript page is from al-Kindi's *On the Art of the Composition of Melodies.* Among his other talents, al-Kindi was an accomplished musician who strongly believed in the healing power of music.

MUSIC

Al-Kindi wrote eight known texts on music. They were titled *On Harmony (Al Kubra fi l-Ta'lif)*, *On the Arrangement of the Tunes Indicating the Nature of the Heavenly Bodies and on the Similarity of Harmony (Tartib al Nagham al-Dallah ala Taba'i' al-Ashkhas al-Aliyah wa Tashabuh al-Ta'lif)*, *Introduction to the Art of Music (L-Madkhal ila Sina'at al-Musiqi)*, *On the Harmony of Sounds (Al-Iqa)*, *On the Art of the Composition of Melodies (Khabar Ta'lif al-Alhan)*, *On the Art of Poetry* (poetry often was sung) *(Sina'at al-Shi'r)*, *On the Parts of Knowledge in Music (Alza' Khabariyyah fi l-Musiqa)*, and *A Short Treatise on the Composition of Tunes and the Making of Lutes (Mukhtasar al-Musiqa fi Ta'lif al-Nagham wa Sina'at al-Ud Alla fahu li-Ahmad ibn al-Mu'tasim)*. Al-Kindi played music, developed musical theory, and could even make his own instruments. That would be like a pop singer today generating the mathematical formulas behind the study of music, writing and playing songs, and then building his or her own guitar. Such was the remarkable talent of al-Kindi.

In his works, al-Kindi determined that notes combine to produce harmony. These notes, in turn, have specific pitches. He said that pitch can determine whether a note is pleasant to the ear. For example, he discovered that notes that are too low or too high because they do not reach the intended pitch are unpleasant. Harmony resulted when notes were combined at just the right pitch and frequency.

Al-Kindi also combined his knowledge of medicine with his music studies. Through observation and sheer educated guesswork, he theorized that sound produces waves in the air. He indicated that these waves hit the eardrum and the vibration of the air movement was what resulted in sound. Many centuries later, scientists largely proved al-Kindi's theory on sound waves to be correct.

CALLIGRAPHY

Imagine what life was like in the ninth century. Telephones, televisions, and computers obviously had not been invented yet. Even electricity, which provides reliable light in the evenings, was many centuries away from being discovered and used. Music, the arts, and the written word provided most entertainment. As such, all three were highly cherished and viewed as sacred, especially the written word. Printing

This page from al-Qazwini's *Marvels of Things Created and Miraculous Aspects of Things Existing* bears a portrait of a scribe, perhaps Sayyid Husayn Yazdi, who signed the undated manuscript. (The page contains a colophon, with key publishing information about the book.) Skilled in calligraphy, scribes were in high demand and were respected professionals in al-Kindi's lifetime.

ومنه والحمد لله رب العالمين والصلوة والسلام

علي خير خلقه محمد

وآله وصحبه اجمعين

تمت بالخير علي الضعيف

سيد حسين يزدي

Al-Kindi's Private Life

The only information about the private life of al-Kindi comes from the writings of later Arab writers. These accounts vary, and it is thought that some men were jealous of al-Kindi or wished to discredit his work because Islamic fundamentalists did not always accept it. Based on multiple accounts, however, a picture does emerge of his life. He was born into a wealthy, prominent family, so writings that claim that he had a luxurious house and garden were probably true. It was also said that he owned many exotic animals. Given al-Kindi's interest in all things from the natural world, that may have been true. Most reports describe him as being a very quiet man to the point of being aloof. One anecdote, for example, mentions that he lived near a wealthy merchant. When asked about al-Kindi, this merchant did not even know anything about al-Kindi's work, which would have been recognized by others during his lifetime. It is therefore likely that al-Kindi was a modest, quiet man. But he was also described as having a great sense of humor. That would seem likely, since a lot of wit derives from knowledge, irony, and the ability to entertain, all of which he must have excelled at given his popularity as a teacher and author. Some other accounts mention that he had at least one son. Al-Kindi lived to a ripe old age, especially by ninth-century standards. Historians believe that he had a happy life at home, which was augmented by his success at work.

presses did not churn out books. Instead, they were painstakingly copied and handwritten, often with special writing styles. Artistic, stylized, or elegant handwriting and lettering is called calligraphy.

Most early cultures practiced calligraphy and supported scribes who copied important texts, which usually were religious works such as the Bible or the Qur'an. The copying of the Qur'an was made possible due to the invention of the north Arabic script in northeast Arabia in the fifth century. It spread to the West, where it came into the hands of the Quraysh tribe, which was the aristocratic tribe to which the prophet Muhammad belonged.

Calligraphic styles at the time were considered either to be "dry" or "moist." Similar to the warm/cold/wet descriptions of medicine, these terms referred more to abstract ideas behind the writing. Dry styles tend to be more clear and plain, while wet styles tend to have rounder shapes and more artistic flourishes. When al-Kindi re-created Greek works or his own, he used these writing styles. As a result, many of his texts are not only interesting to read, but they also exist as works of art. Arabic writing by its nature has a beautiful, artistic look to it, especially when compared to the more linear forms of written English. With the flowing motions and deft brushstrokes of famous calligraphers such as al-Kindi, the beauty of the writing takes on a whole new level because it can be appreciated for its appearance as well as its content.

CRYPTANALYSIS

A cryptogram is some form of communication that is conveyed by a secret or a code. It also refers to any figure or representation that has a hidden meaning. The art of breaking these codes and secrets is called cryptanalysis. Today, the field mainly deals with issues of international security or protection of high-tech data, such as movies on DVDs. Some commercial CDs and DVDs cannot be copied because the information on them was encrypted in a secret code that most home computers cannot read. During World War I and World War II, codes were also often used when military leaders communicated in secret, just in case the letter or signal was intercepted by the enemy.

In ninth-century Arabia, cryptanalysis primarily referred to deciphering books from other countries. Today's readers take it for granted that most major books from around the world have been translated into familiar languages. Al-Kindi did not have this benefit. In many cases, he had to figure out a written language with little, if any, prior instruction in that tongue.

Today, many experts on cryptanalysis credit al-Kindi and the Arabs for starting the field of study. Al-Kindi wrote at least a few manuscripts on the subject, which perhaps were the first of their kind. Portions of them reveal how al-Kindi probably approached a foreign manuscript. He would study the characteristics of letters and determine how frequently

This is the first page of al-Kindi's manuscript *On Deciphering Cryptographic Messages*. It details the scholar's groundbreaking method of translating texts in foreign languages by analyzing the characteristics and frequency of the letters.

they occurred in the text. In a way, this logic was not much different from the manner in which he studied how different pitches can result in harmony. He then would study the length of the overall text to get a full measurement of the occurrence of individual letters.

Next, al-Kindi said it was necessary to create associations between words or letters. He might know some words or phrases in the language, so he would see how these sections fit into the rest of the unknown text. For words that he did not know, he would map out how letters combined with each other in groups of two or three letters. Finally, to prove his point, he took a text consisting of 3,667 letters and broke it down according to his theories. It was in this manner that many of the greatest works of the ancient world were passed down to different cultures and to different generations.

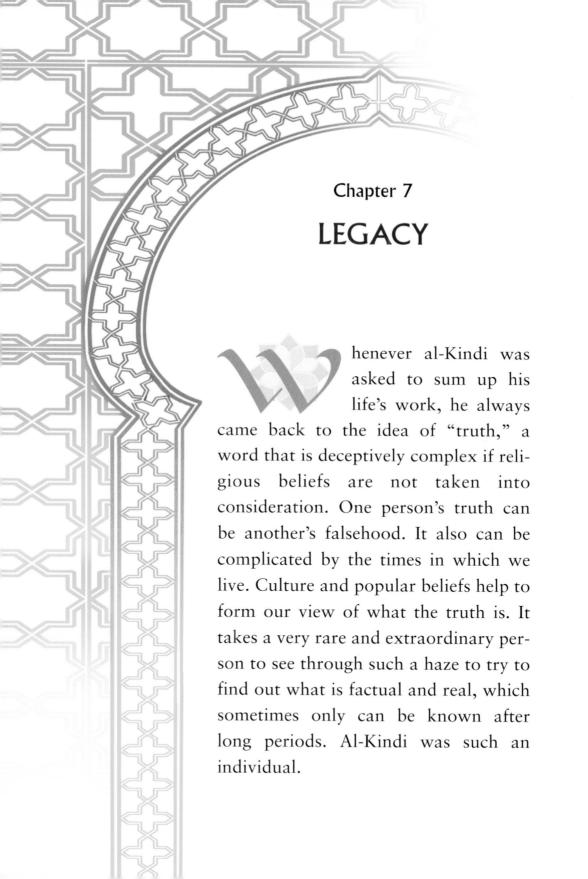

Chapter 7

LEGACY

Whenever al-Kindi was asked to sum up his life's work, he always came back to the idea of "truth," a word that is deceptively complex if religious beliefs are not taken into consideration. One person's truth can be another's falsehood. It also can be complicated by the times in which we live. Culture and popular beliefs help to form our view of what the truth is. It takes a very rare and extraordinary person to see through such a haze to try to find out what is factual and real, which sometimes only can be known after long periods. Al-Kindi was such an individual.

Issued in 1994, this Syrian stamp honors the intellectual genius of al-Kindi. Although virtually unknown in the West, al-Kindi is highly revered in Muslim and Arab countries.

There is no question that al-Kindi was a devout Muslim of Arabic heritage. He brought his impressive heritage and the legacy of scholarly Arabic thought into his teachings and writings. He also respected the "foreign sciences," meaning the work and theories of the ancient Greeks, the Indians, and the educational output of other societies and races. His work bridged the Arabic Islamic traditions with those of Western scientists and philosophers. Considering the political divide that many people believe now exists between the Middle East and the West, al-Kindi and his work should serve to inspire us all as to what is possible if we only take the time to respect other cultures and how they envision the truth.

Time often makes fact clear from fiction. Early societies believed without a doubt that the earth was flat and that our planet was the center of the universe. The evidence collected since then, with the benefit of better technologies, shows that they were wrong. Al-Kindi was not always right, since he lacked such technologies. His views on the origin of certain diseases, like epilepsy, for example, have been disproven, as have some of his findings concerning astronomy. He was often right, however, and his methods were startlingly modern.

Doctors and scientists today marvel at how his thinking mirrors modern logic and scientific experimentation. This passage from his *Treatise on the Efficient Cause of the Flow and Ebb (L-Atharayn al-Mahususayn bi l-Ma)* sounds like it could have been written by a twenty-first-century scientist:

> One can also observe by the senses . . . how in consequence of extreme cold air changes into water. To do this, one takes a glass bottle, fills it completely with snow, and closes its end carefully. Then one determines its weight by weighing. One places it in a container . . . which has previously been weighed. On the surface of the bottle the air changes into water, and appears upon it like the drops on large porous pitchers, so that a considerable amount of water gradually collects inside the container. One then weighs the bottle, the water and the container, and finds their weight greater than previously, which proves the change.

This same use of reason and logic is apparent in al-Kindi's philosophical writings. His conclusions always supported the teachings of Islam, but the methods that he drew upon to reach these conclusions were rooted in science, math, and principles accepted by many other cultures and faiths. It is little wonder that al-Kindi is being rediscovered in the twenty-first century by scholars from around the world because his words often speak a truth that can reach all of us.

TENTH-CENTURY RECOGNITION

In addition to his modern appeal, al-Kindi received praise from scientists and scholars closer to his own lifetime. A biographical note in the text *The Extract (Al-Muntakhab)* by tenth-century scholar Ibn Qudaamah lavished great praise on al-Kindi and his work. Ibn Qudaamah wrote:

Abu Yusuf Ya'qub ibn Isahq al-Kindi was the first to distinguish himself among the Muslims in philosophy and all its branches, and in the exact sciences and every thing connected with them, as well as by his familiarity with the sciences of the Arabs and his excellence in humanities like grammar and poetry, astrology, medicine, various arts and sciences: virtues which are seldom united in a single individual.

He added,

The list of his books exceeds one quire of paper [24 sheets] folded . . . He is the first among the Muslims to introduce this form of writing which was later followed by the succeeding [generations of scholars] among the Muslims. During the days of al-Mamun those who acquired name and fame before him were mostly Christians who had adopted in their works the old style of writing.

INSPIRATION FOR OTHER ARABIC SCHOLARS

As a well-known Persian philosopher, scientist, and even an ophthalmologist who wrote about optics, al-Kindi composed works that would have been required reading

for generations of Arab students in the decades following his death. Some of these later students became famous scholars of many disciplines in their own right. Al-Kindi inspired the works of such eminent philosophers and scientists as Averroes (1126– 1198), Avicenna (980–1037), and Alhazan (ca. 965–1038). Some historians today think that these men overshadowed al-Kindi. While they may have added or even improved upon some of al-Kindi's ideas, it is important to remember that they had the benefit of the additional technological and philosophical advances that developed over time. For his particular place in time, al-Kindi stands out as perhaps the greatest thinker and originator of ideas, according to many modern historians.

ACKNOWLEDGMENT IN THE MIDDLE AGES AND BEYOND

In the sixteenth century, the Italian physician and mathematician Gerolamo Cardano (1501–1576) wrote that

Entitled *Avicenna—The "Persian Galen,"* this twentieth-century American painting shows Avicenna working on a manuscript. The leading physician and medical scholar of his age, he wrote the *Canon of Medicine*, which was the primary text in European medical schools for centuries. Galen, to whom Avicenna is compared in the title, was the leading medical authority in ancient Greece.

This is an aerial view of al-Kindi Plaza in Riyadh, Saudi Arabia. Completed in 1986, the plaza includes a mosque, a library, a garden, government offices, a courtyard, and a public square. Al-Kindi's grand stature in Muslim history and scholarship lends a degree of prestige to buildings, events, and awards named in his honor in Muslim countries.

al-Kindi possessed one of the best minds of all known history. During this period, some of al-Kindi's works also were translated into Latin. As a result, many scientists and philosophers from Europe and around the world were introduced to his work.

Al-Kindi threw open the door to Islamic philosophical thought, meaning that he inspired numerous Muslims to think about the Qur'an and its teachings in a new light that could generate discussion and debate. Because of this, and because of his remarkable contributions to the arts and the sciences, the twentieth century saw renewed interest in his work. Since the 1940s, efforts have been made to locate, restore, and translate his works for the sake of the public. Perhaps little changes over time, especially the quest for truth, since that is precisely what al-Kindi sought.

TIMELINE

circa 470–399 BC

The life of Socrates.

ca. 428–347 BC

The life of Plato.

384–322 BC

The life of Aristotle.

146 BC

Rome conquers Greece, which marks an end to most Greek scholarship from the ancient world.

AD 400

Tribe of Kindah becomes known as a powerful, integrated group.

570

The prophet Muhammad is born.

610–632

The prophet Muhammad experiences revelations from the angel Gabriel that lead to the rise of Islam.

632

Muhammad dies.

641

The city of Kufa is founded.

780

Al-Khwarizmi is born.

786

Al-Rashid comes to power.

ca. 800

Al-Kindi is born.

813

The rule of al-Mamun begins.

847

Al-Mutawakkil comes to power and, with the Banu Musa brothers, later persecutes al-Kindi.

ca. 866

Al-Kindi dies.

1550

Physician and mathematician Gerolamo Cardano states that al-Kindi was one of the twelve most influential men in the history of the world.

1940s–present

Works of al-Kindi's previously thought to have been lost begin to surface.

GLOSSARY

alchemy A medieval science with the goals of changing metals into gold, discovering a single cure for all disease, and prolonging human life.

anthropologist Someone who studies people (past and present) and the way they live.

astrology The study of the effects of the position and movements of the planets have on events on Earth and human behavior.

astronomer Someone who studies the sun, moon, planets, stars, and other heavenly bodies.

atheism The belief that there is no god.

banish To expel someone from a community.

caliph A successor to Muhammad.

calligraphy Stylized, artistic handwriting.

creatio ex nihilo A Latin phrase that means "creation out of nothing," usually in reference to how God may have created the universe.

cryptanalysis The study of secret codes in letters, words, or images.

dogma A doctrine that is accepted as absolute truth, even in the absence of proof.

eminent Distinguished, great, or famous.

ethics The branch of philosophy concerned with moral values and rules; a set of moral principles.

Fertile Crescent A semicircle of fertile land that stretches from part of the Mediterranean to the Persian Gulf; agriculture may have begun there.

fundamentalist One who maintains a strict observance of a religion's founding principles.

harmony The combination of certain musical notes to produce a pleasant sound, such as a chord.

heretical In violation or opposition to the official doctrine or teachings of the church.

Hinduism One of the world's major religions; the dominant religion of India and South Asia.

Islam A religious faith that includes belief in one God, known as Allah, and a belief that Muhammad was his prophet.

metaphysics A part of philosophy that concerns the nature of reality, often in terms of theological views.

Muslim Someone who follows Islam.

Qur'an The holy book of followers of Islam.

nomadic Mobile: refers to a way of life in which a group of people move from place to place and have no permanent home.

observatory A building designed and equipped for studying the stars.

Persia A former empire that used to include parts of what
    now forms southwest Asia.

philosophy All learning aside from technical subjects and
    the arts.

physics The study of matter, energy, and their interactions.

polygamy The state of being married to two or more people
    at the same time.

posology A branch of medicine that al-Kindi practically
    invented that deals with the dosages of drugs.

simultaneously Happening at the same time.

solitude The state of being alone.

theology The study of religion.

tribe A social group that can consist of several families and
    clans that live together, along with their servants and any
    adopted individuals.

FOR MORE INFORMATION

Islamic Bookstore.com
2040-F Lord Baltimore Drive
Baltimore, MD 21244-2501
(410) 265-0020
Web site: http://www.islamicbookstore.com

Middle East International
1 Gough Square
London EC4A 3DE
England
(44) 207-832-1330
Web site: http://www.meionline.com

Middle East Media Guide
Sandstone FZ-LLC
Office 119, 2nd Floor
Building 2
Dubai Media City
P.O. Box 72280, Dubai
United Arab Emirates
Web site: http://www.middleeastmediaguide.com

Middle East Research and Information Project
1500 Massachusetts Avenue NW
Suite 119
Washington, DC 20005
Web site: http://www.merip.org

WEB SITES

Due to the changing nature of Internet links, the Rosen Publishing Group, Inc., has developed an online list of Web sites related to the subject of this book. This site is updated regularly. Please use this link to access the list:

http://www.rosenlinks.com/gmps/kind

FOR FURTHER READING

Ali, Maulana Muhammad. *The Holy Quran*. Wembley, England: Ahmadiyya Anjuman Ishaat, 1983.

Allen, William, and Don Belt. *The World of Islam: The History, Culture and Religion Through the Lens of National Geographic*. New York, NY: Simon and Schuster, 2001.

Armstrong, Karen. *Islam: A Short History*. New York, NY: Random House Publishing Group, 2002.

Awde, Nicholas, and Samano Putros. *The Arabic Alphabet: How to Read It*. New York, NY: Kensington Publishing Corporation, 1987.

Lunde, Paul. *Islam: Faith, Culture and History*. New York, NY: DK Publishing, 2002.

Walsh, Kieran. *Iraq*. Vero Beach, FL: Rourke Publishing, 2004.

Williams, Brian. *Aristotle*. Chicago, IL: Heinemann Library, 2002.

BIBLIOGRAPHY

Al-Allaf, Mashhad. "Theory of Knowledge According to al-Kindi." Islamic Philosophy Online. Retrieved April 2005 (http://www.muslimphilosophy.com/kindi/default.htm).

Al-Razik, Abd Mustafa. *Khamsah Min Alam al-Fikr al-Islami: al-Kindi, al-Farabi, al-Mutanabbi, Ibn al-Haytham, Ibn Taymiyah*. Beirut, Lebanon: Dar al-Katib, 1978.

Atiyeh, George. *Al-Kindi: The Philosopher of the Arabs*. New Delhi, India: Kitab Bhavan, 1994.

Fluegel, Gustav Lebrecht. *Al-Kindi Genannt der Philosoph der Araber: Ein Vorbild Seiner Zeit und Seines Volkes*. Leipzig, Germany: Brockhaus, 1857.

Ivry, Alfred. *Al-Kindi's Metaphysics*. Albany, NY: State University of New York Press, 1974.

Nouha, Stéphan. *Mathématique et pharmacologie dans l'Œuvre Pharmaceutique du Médecin-Philosophe Arabe al-Kindi*. Lille, France: Université de Lille, 1999.

Sharif, M. M. *A History of Muslim Philosophy*. Lahore, Pakistan: Pakistan Philosophical Congress, 2002.

INDEX

About the Author

Tony Abboud is a news journalist and an author of educational materials for such publishers as the *Princeton Review*. As a writer Abboud has covered issues related to Arabic culture and East-West relations for the past five years.

About the Consultant

Munir A. Shaikh, Executive Director of the Council on Islamic Education (CIE), reviewed this book. CIE is a non-advocacy, academic research institute that provides consulting services and academic resources related to teaching about world history and world religions. http://www.cie.org.

Photo Credits

Cover, p. 57 Courtesy of MuslimHeritage.com; p. 7 Image from "The Roots of Consciousness," by Jeffrey Mishlove, permission granted by the author; pp. 10–11 Map by András Bereznay, http://www.historyonmaps.com; p. 13 © Bethune Carmichael/Lonely Planet Images; pp. 16, 61 Bibliothèque Nationale de France; pp. 18, 26 Freer Gallery of Art, Smithsonian Institution, Washington, D.C.: Gift of Charles Lang Freer, F1929.72 (p. 18), F1908.261a-b (p. 26); p. 19 © The British Museum/HIP/The Image Works; p. 21 © The British Library: Or. 2936 f.173; pp. 22, 63, 70, 86 background tiles courtesy of Mosaic House, New York; pp. 23, 41, 71 The Granger Collection, New York; pp. 29, 37 Institute of Oriental Studies, St. Petersburg, Russia/Bridgeman Art Library; pp. 32, 34, 64 Scala/Art Resource, NY; p. 37 (inset) © Mary Evans Picture Library/The Image Works; p. 42 SEF/Art Resource, NY; pp. 45, 54 Erich Lessing/Art Resource, NY; p. 47 Alfred L. Ivry, Intro & Commentary "Al-Kindi's Metaphysics: A Translation of Ya'qub ibn Ishaq al-Kindi's Treatise 'On First Philosophy,'" SUNY Press, Albany, 1974; p. 51 Topkapi Palace Museum, Istanbul, Turkey/Bridgeman Art Library; p. 58 © The British Library: Or. 8069 f. 9v; p. 66 The Art Archive/ Bodleian Library, Oxford, England, Elliott 340 folio 92; p. 73 The Bodleian Library, University of Oxford, England, MS. Huntington 214, title page; p. 76 © The British Library: Or. 9033 f. 60r; pp. 78–79, 96 Courtesy Pfizer Inc, images provided by National Library of Medicine; p. 82 © The British Library: Or. 2361 f. 165r; p. 85 Courtesy National Library of Medicine; p. 89 Suleymaniye Library, Turkey, Document No. 4832 First Page; p. 92 1994 stamp, Syria/Stamp Courtesy Magan Stamps; p. 98 Courtesy of the Aga Khan Trust for Culture.

Designer: Les Kanturek; Editor: Wayne Anderson; Photo Researcher: Gabriel Caplan